Pretty for a black girl!

Compliment or Insult?

Aisha Curry

authorHOUSE®

AuthorHouse™
1663 Liberty Drive, Suite 200
Bloomington, IN 47403
www.authorhouse.com
Phone: 1-800-839-8640

First published by AuthorHouse 4/7/2009

ISBN: 978-1-4389-5410-3 (e)
ISBN: 978-1-4389-5409-7 (sc)

Printed in the United States of America
Bloomington, Indiana

This book is printed on acid-free paper.

Dedication

I wanted to dedicate this book to my husband. He is my best friend, and he encouraged me to write this book. He was a active listener and very patient over the course of time. There were many late nights when I would read things to him, and he would never have a problem staying up a little late just to hear what I had to say. He is very supportive of me and very respectful as well. He always lets me know that I am a beautiful black woman inside and out. He is a great black man and great father he is a much laid back and non judgmental person. Honey I love you and thank you for encouraging me.

Your best friend and wife, Aisha

Acknowledgments

First and foremost, I would like to thank GOD, because without him nothing is possible. GOD makes a way out of no way, and I'm grateful for that. God has been good to my husband and me, and that's where I would like to thank my other half; he is my rock and my sunshine. I am so proud of him. He is living his dream and supporting our family of six. He has been supportive of me when I doubted myself; I love him. He is a strong black man and a mighty man of GOD. He is truly one of a kind. I love that I am spending my life with him. I would like to thank my pastor and first lady for the wisdom and teachings that they have enriched in my life. How can you write an acknowledgment and not thank your mother? Mom, you're the best. Thank you for raising me to be the woman that I am today. Thank you for the sacrifices you made for my sister and me; you are a remarkable human being, you have so much wisdom to share, and so much of your heart you give. I love you. Dad, you are such a kind, hard -working, compassionate man. You show so much love to your daughters and your grandkids. Thank you for always helping me whenever I called on you. I love you. Sis, I want you to know how proud I am of you. You are a strong black woman with a lot of class raising my beautiful niece and nephew. You are an inspiration to young black single women. I love you. To my step sisters, KeKe and Marcie. I love you. Keep striving girls. To my sister cousins, Devan and Danyell. I can't just call the two of you cousins, we were raised as sisters. I love you. My children keep me going. I love my kids; they are such a delight. Patrick, you're an intelligent, sweet boy. Thanks for always helping your mommy. Sienna, that smile of yours brightens my day; you always make me laugh. Raeyvn and Raquel, you are a joy. You have so much personality; you keep me laughing. Samara, who is my goddaughter, you are a very sweet girl. I love all of you. My great-grandmother, Lil Mama, who told me that if you love yourself and you're happy with yourself, it's much easier to love others, I will always keep you in my heart. To my grandmother Pat for being such a strong black woman. You keep the family at the edge of their seats. You are a character and I love you. I have always watched my uncles, Glenn and Danny. I have learned a lot from the two of them. When they didn't think that I was paying attention, I was. I watched how they treated their wives, my sweet aunts. I watch them be good strong black men, being committed and not giving up on their family, being what a man is supposed to be. It took me quite a while to write such a short book. I would begin and stop so many times, because I was so worried about what other people thought of me. Some people like to talk, assume, and pass judgments on you as if they really know you. People will try hard to make your life miserable if you let them. Thank God I was able to divert my feelings and keep striving to be me. When I needed someone to talk to, my mother-in-law Cassandra was always there to listen and give good advice. To my cousin Chelewa, for being so family oriented. I love that about you. Thank you for playing cupid and introducing me to the man that I share my life with. I love you, girl. To one of my oldest friends, Jacques, who led me to Christ and was very persistent I might add, and for introducing me to his lovely wife Racey, who is now my sister in Christ. To my girls Yoli, Mia, Michelle, and Jazz, we have some stories to tell ladies, we can entertain ourselves for hours by reminiscing. I love each one of you; we all have our own special bond. To my cousins, Porshe and Tyson, I like to call them the power couple. I love you guys. Thanks, to my You Tube subscribers who let me know how important this issue is. I know I could keep on going but we have a book to read people, so please don't get made if I left you out, I have too many family members and friends. I love you all, and love having you as a part of my life.

Table of Contents

Introduction

This book is for open-minded Individuals; it's not intended to upset anyone. I am just expressing my view on being a black woman. Being a black man or woman, somehow you are always reminded that you are a black man or a black woman, not just a man or a woman. America's standard of beauty has always been skewed. The ideal race and weight, although trivial, is subjective. I want to help women who feel dispirited and deflated. Black women who are torn between what people determine what is and is not beautiful. Who have been robbed from any confidence they once had. To women, looking in the mirror and saying to themselves "I can't possibly be pretty, I'm too dark, my hair is too short, too nappy, my nose is too big, I'm too fat, or too skinny". This book is for you. to show you that you are not alone. This book is for you, to tell you that you are BEAUTIFUL. I want you to speak it. Read it, walk it, talk it, breathe it and, most importantly, believe it. This book is for all the black women in the world, and to be informative to men and inspiring to all women of every nationality. It's also to be informative to those who are uniformed of this issue.

You will read a really brief description of my childhood and where I grew up. I will share many stories with you about different situations I have been in. You will hear commentary from black men and women and from women of other races and their views on black women. You will also take a quick journey though history. This topic has been surfacing in my mind and heart for years. This book is relatively short and to the point. I hope you enjoy it. All in all, you will find out why I am sick of being told I am "pretty for a black girl".

Let's diminish ugly mindsets and replenish them with a new mind.

Aisha Curry

Chapter One

Childhood

"Childhood is the most beautiful of all life's seasons"

-unknown author

It's funny just how much you can remember from your childhood. I can still recall the preschool experiences I had with my teacher and how she treated me. I can remember many instances such as these. One day our teacher was teaching us how to tie our shoes. As she demonstrated this to us, I waited anxiously with excitement, because I knew how to do this already. So after the demonstration, I raised my hand to show her, and when I tied my shoes for her, I was then sent to a corner in the classroom for the rest of the day. I couldn't understand what I did wrong. I thought that she would be proud of me, but instead she wasn't and I was in trouble.

This same teacher, within the next couple of weeks, began to teach us how to write our first names, and it just so happened that I also already knew how to write my first and last name. What can I say—my mother spent a lot of time teaching me at home. Anyhow, in class we were to write our names on our desks. Each day, when we entered our classroom,

I would write my first and last name, and the teacher would mark out my whole name with a red marker each day. I didn't understand why, so one day I told my mother what the teacher had been doing to me every day. My mother was so upset; she immediately went to the school to find out exactly what had been going on. When my mother confronted the teacher, she asked her about her actions and the teacher replied, "Well, Aisha is doing things and we're not on that, at this point." My mother was furious because this woman was trying to break my self-esteem as a young child and make me feel inferior for being a little advanced. It was then, when my mother saw another child's desk with their first and last name on it, and it was not crossed out with a red marker. This other child just happened to be Caucasian, and did I mention that I was the only black child in my classroom?

I probably was the only black child at my school, so my mother knew right away that this was a racial issue. My mother tells me now that there were other issues going on as well that she wasn't ecstatic about, but these are just some of the things that I remember.

The city, Fremont, in which we lived in was located in Northern California. It was a predominantly white town and they weren't really receptive to black people in the community, so it wasn't too much of a shock to my mother. I was immediately pulled out from that school and then began a private catholic school education.

I was a very friendly little girl. I didn't pay much attention to my color, nor to anyone else's for that matter. Seriously, I didn't even realize that I was black. One afternoon I was at the neighborhood park with my father, and when I came home I was very excited because I had made a new friend. My mother said she can't recall why she asked me this question, but she did. She said, "Was your friend black or white?" and I replied, "Oh, she was white, just like me." My mother thought that was so funny to her, because of my innocence of not knowing my ethnicity, and it was then when my mother told my father, "Okay, it's time for the talk about our heritage and background."

My mother is a beautiful fair-complected woman. She is proud of her culture and taught us how to be proud of our heritage and who we are. She educated my sister and me on our history and ancestry. My mother felt that it was important for us to know who we are and where we came from, and I thank her for that because I believe it builds character. Not only does my mother have very fair skin, but my father and sister do as well. I can recall, around the tender age of ten, my peers would always ask me, "Why is your family lighter than you?" This is when I began to notice that skin color mattered to a lot of people. I always was compared to my sister because I was a little darker, as if I was the ugly duckling or the less fortunate one. It's as if we break down our levels of blackness to fractions of a hue, which is quit sad. Someone is either too dark or not dark enough to be black.

My family is pretty diverse. We have Caucasians and Cherokee Indians in our genealogy. I also have aunts who are Hispanic and Filipino, so growing up I was surrounded by many different ethnicities. I am appreciative for that because I believe it helped me to be as open minded as I am today.

I grew up in Fresno, California; Fresno is the sixth-largest city in California and the largest inland city in the state. Fresno is in the central valley, between San Francisco and Los Angeles. Caucasians make up 50 percent of Fresno; 39 percent are Hispanics or Latinos of any race; 11 percent are Asian; 1.5 percent are Pacific islanders; and 8.36 percent are African

Americans. I feel it's relevant to give you the demographics of where I'm from because some people will have never heard of or will know nothing about some of the things that are talked about in this book , but it's all based on the environment in which they live.

I grew up on the west -side of Fresno. My first day at the neighborhood school in this town was quite different (incommensurable) from my experiences in Fremont. When I first started elementary school at Mary McLeod Bethune, I was in the fourth grade. The kids would laugh at me and say I talked white; I was so clueless to what they meant by this. The moment I got home I asked my mom "Why are the kids at school saying I talk like a white girl." She chuckled a little bit and said "Honey you just have a really good vocabulary and you're a product of your environment, that's all. There is nothing wrong with the way you talk."

I grew to be very fond of that school and that neighborhood most of all. On my block, all the kids in the surrounding neighborhoods would play outside just about all day, until our parents called us inside the house. The whole community felt like home – kids were out running around screaming, laughing, riding bikes, playing ball in the street, or my favorite: double dutch. The elderly men and women would be out sitting on their front lawns or porches, reading or watching the children's jubilant faces as they played. There was something called the corner store; even though it was around the corner from most of our homes it was referred to as the corner store. My sister and I would walk to that store just about twice a day if we could. We would be scraping up change we found in the couch, or raiding our mother's empty purse for change to buy our favorite candies. I used to be crazy about this sweet and sour licorice that was sold in a clear container on the counter of the store. I had two family members who lived two houses down on both sides. I had a relative on every other block, more or less, and all my friends were within walking distance. When my husband first came to California and he saw the West side of Fresno, his first perception of it was that movie Boyz in the Hood.

Into my first year of Junior high school, my mom and dad had separated, so we moved across town into a middle class neighborhood and remained on that side of town forever. We never moved back to the west side and things sure were dissimilar.

Throughout my school years, I would experience some racial remarks here and there. I think most of us have, at some point in our life. In high school, I remember that everyone was separated. You would see all the different type of races gathered in groups around the campus. A couple of other girls and I took notice of how there were no black girls on the cheer team or the color guard teams at our school, so we decided to create a stomp team. It was going to be open auditions to anyone who was interested. It just so happened to be all African American girls who joined. My best friend and I soon became interested in the color guard team. We knew that there had been no black girls on the team, but we took a shot and signed up anyway. I was uncomfortable each day on that team. Our instructor ridiculed us for everything that we did, instead of trying to help us and make us feel comfortable. We would get into trouble if we were one minute late coming from stomp practice, but no one else would get into trouble or be yelled at by arriving late from their extracurricular activities.

The other girls on the team didn't make things better. They always had the ridiculous questions about black people, and you would think that they had never met a black person before.

I couldn't believe it. It was during this time that I was first told that I was I was pretty for a black girl. One of the girls on the team came over to me during practice and said that my best friend and I "were pretty for black girls." I just remember thinking to myself *what does that mean?* As time went on, you would think that things would have gotten better, but we were still singled out from the group, and eventually I just stopped going.

Growing up in Fresno, I never experienced anything too brutal regarding racism. I have experienced things such as being followed around a store because they think I'm going to steal or getting pulled over in a vehicle for no reason other than I'm black; things of that nature that I'm sure seem very common among African Americans. I have gotten some racist statements made towards my culture, such as where did you grow up—in the ghetto? Or, niggers need to go back to Africa. How about this one—all black people are on drugs or in gangs. I have seen and heard some awful things regarding racism. People try to act civilized for the most part, but you can tell sometimes just what one is really thinking when he or she looks at you.

Chapter Two

Other women

"As far as I knew white women were never lonely, except in books. White men adored them, black men desired them and black women worked for them"

-Maya Angelou -

I'm sure most of you have gotten those stares, where you know someone is looking at you, and nine times out of ten they are talking about you as well. Such as this ...

I remember this day like it was yesterday. It seemed to be the hottest day of the year; Fresno is well known for its heat. Well, I was picking up some items at the local Target. While I was standing in the checkout line, this woman kept staring in my direction. It became apparent to me that it was me she was looking at. Eventually she approached me and said, "I just wanted to say that you're really pretty for a black girl." I was infuriated. I felt like someone was giving me a piece of chocolate candy and, when I bit into it, it was a nauseating, rotten piece of crap. I hadn't heard this comment since high school. I find myself to be a pretty amiable person; some of my friends say, "Why, that couldn't have been me. I would have told that lady something." Here's my advice to anyone who has said this to someone: This is not a compliment; this is an insult. A compliment would have been, "I think that you are pretty," not I think you're pretty for a black girl. Some other races have a tendency to think that black people are too sensitive to what they call compliments. They say "Can't anyone give praise to an African American without them taking it so personally? Without being criticized or told you are condescending or prejudiced?" My answer is

"yes, but you have to think about what you are saying. We haven't always been treated as equals and still are looked down upon, so treat us according to knowledge and choose your words before you speak:."

This theory is based on wide spectrum of different psychological studies, of which there are many. Some have said that certain characteristics are universally accepted as attractive. To elucidate what that proclamation means is that Caucasians and Asians have less defined features than people of African, East Indian, or Northern American descent. Some people see strong features, such as big nose and big lips, as masculine characteristics, and the lack thereof as feminine. So, men with more prominent features are generally seen as more attractive, and men with less prominent features seen as less attractive. Conversely, the opposite is true of women; stronger features are seen as less attractive. However, people within a given culture agree among themselves about what faces are attractive, and what makes them attractive. They may easily disagree with people in other cultures about certain attributes of beauty. So, in my opinion, the women who said I was pretty for a black girl apparently saw most African American features as not appealing to her standard of beauty. Some say that beauty is based upon symmetry that is said to be what makes a good model. Yet our features have been made a mockery of; we have been compared to looking like monkeys and apes because of our noses, full lips, and darker complexions. I say, let them think what they want; I personally think that having prominent features separates you from the rest and that is beautiful.

I have always been questioned about my ethnicity; people have mistaken me for Ethiopian, Puerto Rican, and even French, depending on what part of the continent I'm on – which is very normal these days, considering the numbers of biracial individuals. I don't think there is anything wrong with asking someone what nationality they are. In fact, I think it's better to ask whenever you're not sure of something; sometimes it's not what you say, it's how you say it. But as my mother says, some things should just never be said, and telling someone that they are pretty for who they are should be one of them. It's astonishing to me just how often I have heard this, or someone else has told me that someone has made that comment to them. More frequently others have told me they get "You're pretty for a dark skinned girl." At one point, it became an inside joke between my husband and me, and he began to understand just what I had been talking about.

My question was and still is "what is pretty for a black girl? Who defines beauty? And whose standards are these?"

1. Pretty for a black girl… To me this means that we are not the norm; that one considers to be black. This generalization falls into images of stereotypes. Very dark skin, Course hair, broad nose, loud, neck popping individuals. These cannot determine every black woman.

2. Who defines beauty? Who says black is not beautiful? Who's to say course hair and broad noses are not beautiful??? I'll tell you.

3. Whose standards are these? America's standards based on Europeans standards of beauty which means white. The media advertisements set standards, and try to define how they perceive beauty. People tend to think, this is the way they have to look to be considered beautiful. Set your own standards. No one can define beautiful because everyone has something beautiful about them.

Being that I have answered these questions, hear is one of the ugliest comments I ever had heard.

One afternoon, my cousin, who is about the same complexion as Halle Berry, was out shopping and a Caucasian girl approached her and said, "Black people are so lucky. You have such a pretty skin color. You don't have to go out and tan like we do to get that color." Before my cousin could reply she then said, "Except for those dark ones; you know those burnt black ones. They look dirty and ugly." My cousin then replied, "That's mean of you to say, because they can't help nor change their skin color." Along with some other words that I won't repeat. My cousin said the girl then tried to clear herself up and change how she had said it. I guess the girl thought because my cousin is a light- skinned woman she wouldn't see any harm in what she said.

How can anyone have the audacity to say this to anyone, especially directly to a woman of color? That's audacious, prejudiced, ignorant, and rude! Who are we to judge as people? GOD created us all in his likeness and image. With society and the media's views on beauty, it seems as if beauty has something to do with light skin or long hair, so I think maybe some women who have these, what some might say qualities or attributes have a burst of confidence that makes them feel that they are better than those who have other characteristics. And these types of women would have agreed with the Caucasian woman and her statement.

On my job a couple of years back, I worked with a majority of whites and Hispanics. Besides myself out of 300-plus employees, there were maybe three blacks. I would hear all the stereotypical comments about black people or get comments about my hair; that it isn't like most black people's hair. I was starting to become desensitized from all the ignorance. For some of you reading this, you know exactly what I'm talking about, and to those who don't quite understand, these are the types of comments we, as black women, encounter all the time in the workplace or at school, where people feel that they can ask you ridiculous questions or make some of the most stereotypical comments. I used to hear the Hispanic girls discuss their skin complexions. I heard one girl ask another why was she was so dark while a Hispanic and she said, "I bet you got teased a lot growing up," and the other girl replied, "Yes I did. They used to always call me the n word." The girls made it very clear that they were lucky not to have dark skin. I was insulted to be in their presence as a black woman. I thought to myself that if they think that her complexion was so despicable, what must they have thought of mine? The funny thing is that that girl with the darker skin was truly the most beautiful among any of those girls who were trying to make her feel bad about herself.

A very dear friend of mine, who happened to be Hispanic, invited me and another one of my friends, who is also African American, to her birthday party, which she was throwing with two other girls. When we arrived at the party, the room was decorated beautifully with saffron, there were people laughing and having a good time. The music was going, Couples were already dancing. My girl friend and I just knew we were in for a good time. As we settled in, it felt like an unwanted spot light was shinning on the two of us. You know that feeling where you're wearing an uncomfortable garment trying to look cute, and your pants are in your butt, but you don't want to pick it out because you're ashamed that someone is looking. That's kind of how it felt, except for the being ashamed part. I just had to finish that that sentence, because I have been there before. Regardless of that, we were the only two black people in the room. It clearly made no difference to me; I'm just giving you a description of the atmosphere. You could just tell that these groups of individuals were not among black people often. The Hispanic men were drawn to my friend and me. They were asking to take pictures with us and again telling us that we were very pretty black girls. Yes, I know this sounds self indulging, but it's how it really was. I was shocked too. Meanwhile, the other women at the party were not too happy with what was going on, and they started giving us mean looks. We were getting tired of the disrespectful attitudes, so I told my friend who invited us that we were leaving and she said, "Don't worry about those girls. They're just jealous." There was going to be an after-party following behind the birthday party, and the other women had asked my friend, "If you come, you're not bringing those black girls, are you?"

I can't imagine what they must have been saying behind our backs. They were devastated to see that yes, the Hispanic men were attracted to us, the black girls.

So I wonder if other women really think that we are not as attractive as them, because they think they are the preferable type. Or are they somehow intimidated by black women and they try to make us feel inferior to make themselves feel better? I don't want anyone reading this to say this girl must have low self-esteem. It's not that at all. I love myself and I love how GOD created me. No one is perfect and like any women, we all struggle with some type of insecurity. It's just so aggravating when people pass judgment and look down on others because of their nationality or background. It's one thing for people to feel a certain way and contain their feelings, but in my experience, people have been expressing themselves very openly and I just can't stand the mindset of, "I'm better than you because I'm lighter than you", or "I'm better than you because you're black and I'm not".

Ponder upon this for a moment. Caucasian women tan because to be really pale is not appealing to most people, and to be really dark skinned is not appealing to most people either. However, I can almost guarantee that a white woman would rather stay pale white than be really dark, and dark skinned woman would prefer to be pale than really dark. It's just the way our society has made it. When I looked up the word black in the Merriam Webster dictionary, the definition of black is "very dark in color," followed by "his face was black with rage," along with "soiled hands black with grime and black magic," none of which are very pleasant. On the contrary, the definition of white is "free from spot or blemish, stereotypical association of good character with northern European descent," along "with purity," none of which are made to be negative.

When did hair become so important to people? I have noticed how women of other ethnicities always tend to pass judgment on black women's hair. If it's nice, they assume it's fake and they say, "Wow, you have good hair!" So the closer your hair is to white people's hair, the better it is? I have a friend who is white. She wears a hair weave and agrees that saying you're pretty for a black girl is ignorant. However, listen to this. Getting back to the hair weave, she asked me is this all my natural hair and when I said yes she said, "Oh, because the black girls where I'm from don't have nice hair. It's short and hard and they always put weaves in their hair to make it long. I just put weaves in my hair to make it thick because my hair is naturally long." Okay now, I'm not trying to talk bad about her, because she didn't mean anything by it, but you can see how women of other ethnicity think. She was not intentionally trying to sound arrogant or rude; like my husband tells me all the time, you can't get made at someone when they don't know any better. It was as if she was saying that it's okay for her to wear a hair weave because she has more hair than the average black women, forgetting or not realizing that I am a black woman. But I guess I was an exception or something. It's almost the same as saying "I'm pretty for a black girl".

One of my favorite artists India Arie wrote a beautiful song that I find to be inspiring to black women, women who have lost their hair due to cancer or alopecia, and women in general. This is the chorus and a verse. It says " I am not my hair; I am not my skin; I am not your expectations no; I am not my hair; I am not my skin; I am a soul that lives within; Good hair means curls and waves, bad hair means you look like a slave "

My point exactly, we are more than our hair and skin color. Readers, if you yourself have never said or thought this way, don't get defensive because I have to remind you that I am only writing about the ones who have.

New York and Miami can be quite a culture shock if you have never been there. There is so much diversity there. I remember the first time I went to meet my husband's family in New York. While staying there, my husband took me to one of his favorite restaurants in Brooklyn. When we were at the restaurant and the waitress came to take our order, she insisted on speaking to me in Spanish. I found it to be a bit odd; I was thinking to myself, *we are in New York, not a different country. Why doesn't she speak English?* A few minutes later, another black woman came into the restaurant, and I overheard her ordering her food in Spanish. It was then that I realized perhaps the waitress thought I was another ethnicity. The black women who had came in was the same complexion as me, however, her nationality was Dominican.

You will see many men and women with very dark complexions and you will sometimes assume that they are black. What I find peculiar is some of them do not like to be considered of African descent. On the other hand, you will find some Spanish people who will say that they are of African descent. When you take a look at history, you will see that slave ships were sent to South America, Central America, and Brazil in the early 1900s. Therefore, there were many Africans there who mixed with the Spaniards and populated their country; so many of them are of African descent. Some of the women I know act as if they are so much better than black women, and if you call them black it's as if you are being degrading to them. They do not want to be black, let alone a Puerto Rican be called a Dominican, or vice versa. They have their own division going about in their culture as well. Although it's not a black or white thing, it is however an issue based on the shade of their skin complexions; they too admire lighter skin. I understand it's important to be proud of your heritage, but at some point it's also important to know that we all come from one race, especially to the ones who are all of color. I find it strange because, at some point, they have faced some prejudice by people as well, but yet some Spanish people are prejudiced towards African Americans. I know where I am from, some carry this prejudice. In Los Angeles around five years ago, I was in Compton, visiting a friend, and we were all hanging out in the front yard. Soon I noticed everyone started scattering to their houses and moving their cars to the back yard. I asked my friend, "What the heck is going on?" He said, "There is a Mexican gang; going around shooting any black person they see on sight." I was flabbergasted. I had no idea that it was so racist between Mexicans and Blacks. Nevertheless, I had heard a few Mexican men/women refer to black people as niggers when I was growing up, and I would be so upset because they were consider a minority just as I was.

I hate to use the term acting black or talking black. What is acting black? Some people might say that this is a ludicrous generalization, but it some cases it's kind of true. When our ancestors were first brought here, they were stripped of their language. So they started speaking differently, to have their own identity, because they had soon forgotten how to speak their native tongue. This is what some may call country, ghetto, and back in the day, nigger talk. Nowadays, I see many people of other races imitating the black culture; hip-hop is generated from the black culture, correct? It's not just music but it's also fashion, and you see all kinds of people enjoying and partaking in this cultural life style. Yet those same individuals would not like you to see them as simulating the black culture. Although they clearly imitate the black culture with the way they talk and dress, not to mention that they love to date our black men. So it's okay to portray characteristics of blacks as long as you're not considered one or referred to as one yourself?

Women are all generally competitive with one another. It's just our nature to want to look nice or nicer than the women to our left or the women on television whom we think our mates are eyeballing. There are so many beautiful women all over this world, and since we are the majority, things tend to get a little testy with women. We shouldn't have to make someone else feel bad because they don't have the same characteristics as we do. I know that this topic can play into any racial group; for example, if a white girl went to a black school and she happened to have a little meat on her bones, she would hear, "You're thick for a white girl." So that statement would be implying that most white women are skinny. I know that other people encounter all types of comments made by closed-minded individuals. I'm aware of that, but I'm a black woman so I'm simply talking from a black woman's point of view.

Women, I know the world can be judgmental when it comes to appearances. As women, we all like to look nice and we try to fit in with the way society views attraction and with what seems to be appealing. We tend to follow trends with our hair and keep up with fashion. We worry about our bodies: if we're too fat or too skinny; if our breasts are too big or too small. And, as women, we want to be judged for our intellect, personalities, and hearts, not for just the way we look. Face it, looks will only get you in the door, but it won't keep you in the house. Some of the most attractive women are porn stars, strippers, and et cetera. They are getting by only on their looks. I am recognizing just how many superficial women there are in the world. Women in this day and age are concerning themselves with looks far too much; if they would only use all that energy on something positive, we wouldn't have so many trivial problems between one another. Focus on the whole you, inner beauty first and foremost. Let's love the skin we are in and be happy for how God made us; let's not pass judgments on others and remember that beauty is in the eye of the beholder.

Chapter Three

Black men

"Black men who have succeeded, have an obligation to serve as role models for young men entrapped by a vicious cycle of poverty, despair, and hopelessness. -Benjamin L. Hooks-

One thing I can't seem to understand is why some of our black men are so judgmental when it comes to black women. This just irritates me beyond belief. I have heard black men say some very cruel and stereotypical comments when it comes to black women, as if they are not black themselves.

We live in a very diverse society. We have more biracial children and couples than ever before. I don't see anything wrong with this, and I am not against interracial dating. I do believe, however, that preferring your own people and background shows how much you love and respect yourself. Loving and respecting yourselves shows how much you can love and respect others. My number one concern with this generation is that I have encountered some men with very ignorant, closed-minded mentalities. I am not, in any way, trying to put down all black men. I know that not all of you are this way. Trust me; I'm married to a good black man. I am only talking about the ones who have made the judgmental comments.

I bet you all thought that the comment ("you're pretty for a black girl") was said only by other men or other women of other ethnicities. Sorry to say, but black men say this also. This is an insult when other races say this to us, and it's a real slap in the face when you say it.

I was dating this black guy, and from what I knew of him, he didn't date black women. I never asked, nor did I care. One evening, we were out walking and he said to me, "I don't normally date black girls, but I always liked you. I think you are smart and pretty." I thought how sweet; everyone is entitled to his or her opinion and preferences. I didn't see any harm in what he had said. So I asked him, "Why don't you prefer black women?" And he said, "Black women have bad attitudes and they like guys who have their pants hanging off their butts, so they're usually not interested in me." I thought to myself, *here we go, another black man categorizing us and assuming that all black women are this way.* I think the bad boy image is in women generally, not just black women. The black single women whom I know want a good man who has potential and something going for him. So here we have it—a young, educated black man who owns his own business is only interested in other women because he thinks that black women all have bad attitudes and only want a certain kind of man. It sounds to me like he has his own insecurities and makes up excuses that leave him limited in the women that he could possibly be dating. I will allow you to draw your own conclusion.

I have heard black men say that most black women are ugly and black women don't take care of themselves. I happened to overhear a black man's opinion on black women. He made the statement that black girls look dirty. He said this to one of his white peers. The ironic thing about this is that, like I said, he's black. Why doesn't he think he's dirty? They also say the majority of black women are overweight; what's considered overweight? Most black women have meat on their bones; we usually are not bone skinny. If it's the weight issue, why are a lot of black men with overweight white women or Spanish women? I think that's just one of the many excuses that are being used.

This is an issue that just makes me sick to my stomach. Why is it that a dark-skinned black man can say he doesn't think that a dark-skinned black woman is pretty? I have heard this one too many times. Their concern for being with someone their own skin color worries them, with the possibility that their potential child will be dark skinned. I know a black man who truly ruined his relationship with his fiancé whom he said he loved, because he didn't want to marry her because he did not want his kids to be dark. For a man to say that, he must not be confident in himself. It sounds to me like an insecurity issue that he had, maybe growing up, when he was teased for his skin complexion. We all know how judgmental people can be, and sometimes it affects people later on down the line, leaving them with a self-esteem problem. Nine times out of ten, if you're dark complected then your mother or father is too. Someone in your family is going to be your color, so what do these men think of their own mothers, sisters, cousins, nieces, and aunts? Are they ugly too? We all need to build one another up, not bring one another down. Society has done a good job at that already. You don't have to have a baby with a woman of another race to have a beautiful baby. Why do some of you feel that black women aren't capable of having beautiful black babies?

If you prefer a woman of another race that is fine; to each his own. I believe you should love the one to whom God has sent you, but you should not do it because you're worried about an image– an image that someone else has molded you to believe is beautiful. Follow your heart. Having a preference is one thing; being biased is another. Love is not judgmental; love is not prejudiced; love should be unconditional. Some men are really conditioned about stereotypes about black women; that we are loud, rude, and ghetto. But what I find so interesting about that is the white and Latin girls they seem to date who act in this manner and yet it's overlooked when they do it. Men, you criticize black women for wearing hair weaves. You say you can't stand a woman with fake hair. Truth is the majority of you like long hair and then, when a girl goes for the natural look, you're still checking out the girl with the long hair. What is so funny to me is when black men say that they can't stand a girl with a hair weave. Then why is it okay that your woman of a different race wears one? Hair these days, to most women, is an accessory; superstars have made this trend very popular, from Paris Hilton to Beyoncé. It's just to be more glamorous. It's just like makeup; some men say they can't stand a woman to wear too much makeup, but then you see that same man eyeballing a woman who is completely fake and made up on television. Like I said, we get criticized for being fake, or ghetto, with artificial hair, but it's okay to be with a woman who tans for her skin color when we have it natural? Isn't that fake? Women who are not of color wear a lot of makeup, in my opinion; I don't know many black women who wear foundation on a daily basis. Nowadays, you will see all kinds of women with fake butts and lip injections. Aren't these some qualities that most black women have naturally? Years ago, black women were teased for having these attributes, but now the world says it's more than okay to have a big butt or full lips. But it seems as if it's more flattering on other women, in most cases.

You see, all women trying to fit into the image that the world finds to be beautiful, so you men should not talk down on black women for doing such, because it's not just us. There are so many creams and surgeries out to improve a woman's body and appearance, and it seems as if women are ready to do anything to look the way that they think will make you admire them.

What I have found to be the number one reason, or what I call excuse, why black men don't date black women is that black women have bad attitudes. In terms of the infamous attitude of the black women, it's us responding to the double negative—that is not only being a woman, but of African descent too—that completely puts us at the bottom of every social hierarchy. Now I'm not trying to make excuses for anyone who is just mean and thinks that they can just say what they want to anyone. I'm talking about all the opposites. There's always a bad apple in a bunch, so not every black women should be considered that bad apple.

Black women are strong. I think that black people in general come from strong backgrounds. Look at your mothers and grandmothers. They are some very strong individuals. Black women for many generations have been trying to hold their households together. Look at the older women in your church. I remember growing up and noticing that more than half of the body of the church were women (where were the black men?). In the late sixties, seventies and early eighties, the view of black women was ugly. The black woman cried a lot and worked hard, often having two, sometimes three, jobs. She was drained, she was hurting, and she was alone. Why? Because black men were in jail, running off, into drugs, or whatever else they could get into. She had too many hard times and yet people treated her like crap. As a young child, you see this, and you began to look elsewhere. Who is not having these hard times, whose mom is not crying, not struggling? You see; black women have to play the roles as the mother and the father in a lot of situations. We survive through hard times because of the natural strength that God gave us.

Black men, you have played a huge role in the molding and shaping of the hardness of black women, and then you don't want to date us because you say we have bad attitudes. Only 36 percent—and what a small percentage that is—of black families stay together. Some black men have a huge problem in commitment. Men back out of relationships when a woman becomes pregnant or when a woman wants to become married. Our family values have fallen by the wayside and we need to get them back. Most black women have the same story—raised by a single parent, usually the mother, father not around; again not saying all, but the majority. So as black women get older, we take all of this with us as adults, and we have got to learn to let things go and give it to God and let him fix us. I know a lot of black women are very independent because of how we were raised. Most of us had to get jobs at a young age, and we helped take care of our households. I know that my mother did; although she had it harder than I did, I too had to do endure some of the same trials. Men, I think you take our independence, our strength, and you make it negative, when I am sure you have had the same story as most of us. Let's face the facts—based on those percentages, black men, you too have more than likely grown up in a single-parent household, so you understand and you saw the struggles.

White people, generally speaking, have it slightly easier than blacks do. Just color alone gives them an advantage most of the time, so the world is already easygoing on them; that makes a difference in itself. I mentioned that only 36 percent of black families stay together. Let's look at the statistics of others: 74 percent of white families and 64 percent of Hispanics have both parents in the home. And again, look at us black people: Only 36 percent have both parents. So I believe this makes and shapes a difference on how one could be in a relationship. We African Americans need to make a change in how we view family life. America, in general, is becoming increasingly terrible in family values. European families and Middle Eastern families really take the time to spend with one another and they embrace their culture. I love the way Europeans close their businesses in the afternoon for a couple of hours. They do this so that they can eat lunch together and spend quality time with one another. I didn't always like the idea; because whenever I wanted to get out of the house and do something, everything was closed– but, when I looked at the bigger picture, I soon began to quickly appreciate it. They do these things, amongst others, which are truly interesting in terms of family time. I pray that we, as a culture, will soon do the same. ;

Someone once questioned me, asking, "What are you talking about? Black men date black women. Statistically, a majority of black men marry black women." And that may be so. There comes a time when a mature man must make changes in his needs and his feelings. There comes a time when he realizes where he comes from and where he is going. What some black men are finding out is, the "other" women, don't have the inner strength to hold it down, when they are sick, when they have hard times, when they can't get by on their looks, when their people look at them funny. These black men are soon realizing that maybe it was all an illusion– That maybe, those strong black women are not so bad after all.

Time and time again, I have heard men say that white women are easier to get along with. They are more submissive than black women, and white women are pushovers. Any strong women, no matter her race, shall not stand for disrespectfulness from a man. Conversely, men before you go around proclaiming that black women are not submissive, let me share with you my thoughts on the word 'submissive'. When I think of the word submissive, I take it quite literally. I see this word as being a direct order from God. Okay there… let me explain; GOD says,

> "Wives, submit yourselves unto your husbands, as unto the lord."And he tells the Husband "husbands, love your wives, even as Christ also loved the church, and gave himself for it;"

So this can be viewed in two ways. First, is this your wife? Second, does she have potential to be your wife? If she is your wife, then you have to make sure you are submitting yourself to God, so that she can submit herself to you, and this takes faith and prayer. If she is someone who you really like, guess what? You still have to submit yourself to GOD first and seek his guidance. You have to be everything that you are supposed to be so that she can respect you first, before submitting to you. Women have to at least respect a man she is submitting to, she doesn't necessarily have to agree with everything or believe he's making right decisions, but she does have to respect them.

My husband is a professional athlete; with his career, we have been blessed to travel to different parts of the world. I find it fascinating to experience different cultures and different lifestyles. One thing that I have found to be the same everywhere we go is the mentality of women. I don't know what it is about an athlete and (or) entertainer that women tend to throw themselves at them as if they're a prize to be won. So generally speaking, from this point of view, the things that I have seen, you wouldn't believe. I can say that women of other ethnicities do, however, throw themselves at black men. Black men seem to be attractive to other races, and I think that the attention they show these men makes them attractive to them or curious, I should say, and how often do these men turn down women? I personally know some white women who do bend over backwards for their man; I mean to the point where I feel sorry for them because a man is never going to tell you to stop once you've gone so far. The truth of the matter is that men and women truly and completely think differently. Women process life by communicating, so typically we want you to listen and we want to be heard. Men are the complete opposite; they are internal creatures. Men are to the point where they see black and white and women see black, grey, off white, white, blue, black; you get my point.

Some men say that black women are picky when it comes to a man. Hmm, well I feel like all men, not just black men, are very picky as to whom they prefer to date. I mean, I know we all have certain likes and dislikes, but when you don't dress nice, smell pleasant, and can barely take care of yourself, why do you act like you are so much better than a decent women who is loving and kind and respectful and has a job and so much to offer? Because she is not your type: light skin, long hair, white, or whatever it is that you think you're looking for.

Society sees most black men as gangbangers or rappers; irresponsible money handlers. They see black women as ghetto loud-mouth women, and when people come across an educated black man or women they give you a pat on the back and say good job, wow this one articulates well and has etiquette. But you will never measure up to be equal. That's just the way some people think, and I know that sounds so 1950s, but it is still this way.

I just want to say to all my brothers out there – I am not trying to degrade you in any way; I can't say that enough. As my husband was reading this he happened to say, "You sound like you're talking down on us black men," but as he continued to read, he then understood just where I was coming from. I'm just calling it how I see it. I just want the ones who pass assumptions on black women to realize that you're hurting us; you're talking bad about us to other men and women of other races. We all need to try and remember where we come from and learn to love and embrace our culture, and if you do see a women, who fits your stereotype, just remember that you don't know her story, and if it frustrates you, then pray for her. Prayer never seems to hurt anyone. I urge you to pray for all people (1 Timothy 2:1–2). Remember God is the creator and author of all our lives, he is love and we shall be the same. I am not, however, trying to justify any bad behavior by women. I just want men to stop putting us all in one category and to stop demoralizing us. I know that we have a ways to go in our own areas, but we have to evaluate ourselves and start to make some adjustments.

Chapter Four

Black Women

"I want history to remember me not just as the first black women to be elected to congress, not as the first black women to have made a bid for the presidency of the United States, but as a black women who lived in the 20th century and dared to be herself."

Shirley Chisholm

My family and I have been out of the United States for a while now and we get bored from time to time. They show the same stuff on television, so often my husband and I reminisce about old movies we used to watch while growing up. I happened to think about that movie *School Daze* directed by Spike Lee, and I thought about that hair shop scene, when it was the light-skinned girls vs. the dark-skinned girls for the majority. They were singing about good or bad hair, wannabees and gigaboos, and it occurred to me that, although it was a movie, that's kind of the way it is in some black communities and even within some of the college sororities. This is slightly how it is in some places; you see college sororities divided up between dark-skinned girls and light-skinned girls. We have been divided since slavery; it's that old conditioned mind frame. I will further explain this in chapter six. It's as if the closer you are to white, the better you are, although it isn't like that in everyone's eyes; in most cases black is just black. My sistas, some of you are guilty of this, thinking you are better because you have light skin or longer hair and for some reason feeling sorry for a dark-skinned woman and saying to yourself that you're lucky. I wish this was something that I haven't heard with my own two ears, but sadly, it is.

Throughout this book I have said that not all people have the mindset of the things that I am talking about, but the reality is that some do, and that's why I am addressing this issue. Some states in the United States are worse than others. To some of my readers, this issue is relevant and they understand. To others, it's not relevant, and they don't understand and it's shocking to them. I have been traveling throughout Europe, and this problem is not just in the United States; it's worldwide. This is something that appears to be popular, and this goes back to high school for me. You would see the mixed girls or light-skinned girls hanging with only each other, and they would call themselves the pretty girls, or they would say they can't have dark-skinned friends because their friends tend to get jealous of them because they got all the attention. Or it could be the opposite; the darker-complected girl gets upset because the lighter girl thinks that she is better than the darker girl and the darker girl gets tired of being overlooked. This may sound childish, and it is. Most of these things happen before maturity kicks in, but unfortunately, some of these mindsets are in-grown in women today. Here I am, writing a book about other races and black men saying ignorant things about black women. It's come time that we must evaluate our selves. Okay;

black women, take your hands from over your eyes. I have addressed everyone else. It is only fair to keep it real in order to prosper. It makes me so despondent that some of you even feel the way you do. It's an enslaved mindset that some of you have and you don't even realize it.

I had a twenty-four-year-old, African American women tell me, "I don't see what's so wrong with someone telling you you're pretty for a black girl." She said, "I get this all the time too. I embrace it and take it as a compliment. At least I know I am attractive to every race, not just black men, so you should be happy you're attractive and you're not one of those unfortunate ugly black girls who are constantly staring me down because they're jealous."

You see, this is what I am talking about. What an arrogant comment. I do not, in any way, take that as a compliment. Like I said before, it's an insult. Why do you have to accept the fact that someone can say you're pretty for a black girl and not just pretty? This is the acceptance of being accepted. Black women justify their beauty to feel more accepted by other races. What I mean by this is, if someone says to you, "You have a nice skin tone. It's better than those really dark girls." and you say, "Oh yeah. Well, I'm mixed. My grandfather's mom's dad was half white" or something of that nature. I'm not saying don't be proud of your heritage, but we all know that most of us are mixed with a little bit of something. I have heard women proclaiming to be something they're not, just to fit in or be accepted a little more. It's okay to be black and beautiful. You don't have to explain your family tree to someone.

This mindset is not just in young women. In high school, my second boyfriend's mother, ugh! She drove me crazy. This woman was so obsessed with color; she was a few shades darker than me. Her son was very light skinned, about the same complexion as Nicole Richie, with green eyes. She talked about nothing more than how cute her son was. That isn't so much what bothered me, even though that was so irritating. It was the fact that she obsessed over this color issue. She would tell me that he had never dated anyone my color before; she blatantly told me she preferred him to date light skinned women. She would say she wanted her grandchildren to be light skinned. What is crazy is that I just said this guy was my second boyfriend in high school, so who's even thinking about kids at this point? Why would she make me feel like I wasn't good enough for him? I used to think *man, she must have a low self esteem about herself* or else she had gone through some things in her life with racism. Although her absurd talk did annoy me, I somehow didn't get too upset with her. It's as if I understood her story without her telling me. What I can tell you is that this relationship did not last long at all. Ironically, soon after we broke up, he sure enough was with… a light skinned girl.

I am aware that every race has a stereotype, but I am only talking about the stereotypes of black women because I can, since I am black woman. We, as black women, have it pretty hard in that department. We are called everything from ugly and ghetto and loud to angry black women and more. We have got to pull it together and take pride in ourselves. As women, we are misconstrued by black men or by men in general. The image that is implanted in their heads is not the image of most of us all.

I personally love being a black woman. I am proud of who I am and I am proud of my culture. I understand things that black women go through. I do feel like we have it harder, like I said before. It's the double negative of being a woman and then being a woman of color. Being a woman, you want to be respected for your mind, not your body. On television, sex sells. Every channel is about something sexual. I don't watch videos too often, but from what I see of them, especially in the rap videos, there are a lot of women being disrespected, showing their bodies and simply looking like sex objects. I know that there are videos of women of other races as well. It's just, very seldom, the main girl in a video is not black and you see a lot of black women half naked shaking their butts in the video. It's as if we are saying, "Do we have your attention now?" We, as black women, should really step back and look at how the media portrays us and should want better.

Let's examine, why? Some men say we have bad attitudes and are not submissive. As I stated before, black women are strong; and we are some very opinionated creatures. Some of us are head strong. I will use myself as an example. I grew up with a father who was in and out of my life, although my stepfather did raise me. Between the drama, I saw men try to mistreat my mother, emotional and physically. I don't know what to say about some of these men from that era. The thing about my mom was that she was, in no way, going to stand for mistreatment by any man; you only got one chance and when they screwed that up, that was it. She is very strong-willed and outspoken but very compassionate at the same time. In any event, I grew up knowing that nothing was going to be handed to me. In high school, as soon as I could get a working permit, I did, in order to have some of the things I desired. Right after high school, I had a decent paying job and my own apartment. I didn't waste any time. So I didn't rely on a man; I rarely even trusted a man. I felt like every time I let one get close to me, he either had hurt my mom, or my sister and me. My brother and I were extremely close and we shared a very special relationship; to my torment and disbelief, he tragically lost his life at twenty years of age. My spirits were so down; I felt an excruciating pain. I felt like again another man I loved had left me. So I was guarded; I carried a lot of this pain with me through previous relationships. I am now on a road to self-recovery, learning about myself and learning to let go of such pain. It's not fair for anyone to carry their baggage, blame, hurt, or guilt into a relationship. Even if every person you try to respect and uphold has treated you badly, it's a new relationship and everyone deserves the benefit of doubt. Just like anyone in court is innocent until proven guilty. What I am trying to get at is this. We do have to try to be more respectful and submissive to our mates or potential mates. If we want them to be right, we have to be right. That's why I put all my love and understanding in God, and try to abide by his word; because He is my strength and has helped me understand so much in life. Remember that being submissive to a man does not strip you from yourself, your needs, wants, and aspirations. If a man loves you the way he should, he won't allow such domineering behaviors to occur. Men need to be RESPECTED more than loved. Hey! You're never going to find a perfect man; they all have problems. (Giggling). Know that I have addressed this issue, so the men don't feel like I just tried to single them out.

Back to this, light skinned vs. dark skinned mentality. Black women, you are beautiful. Stop worrying about your skin complexion because it does not determine your beauty or your self-worth.

Contemplate this: How many black women do you see hanging out at a beach or swimming during the day. Not many, right? It's not a secret that swimming is not the most favorable thing to do when you're a black women, because of our hair. However, I am not talking about our hair, even though that's a pain in the butt. It's the constant worrying about getting darker, as if it's a crime or if there is something wrong with getting a tan. No one wants to be darker if there is a choice not to be. This goes for black people in general. I had the opportunity to go to a beautiful beach in Tel Aviv, Israel. It was such a beautiful place. The water was so calm and relaxing – the bluest I had ever seen. It was extremely hot. Although it was record-breaking temperature for the area on this day, it felt like a typical summer day in Fresno. This means that it had to be at least 104 degrees, with no breeze and no humidity – just dry desert heat. I personally do not care for that kind of heat. There were absolutely no shaded areas. You could purchase an umbrella to sit under, but it was a lengthy walk from the beginning of the sand to where you could rent the umbrella. I had gone out to this beach with my children and a friend of mine who happens to be white. We were having a good time but an hour passed. I was hot and already ready to go, while my friend was lying out in the sun or sitting in the sand with her son. I was either in the water or underneath the umbrella, trying to keep out of the sun. It was just extremely too hot. I had no reason to want to just lie in the sun. I didn't need a tan.

It was a very different experience than when I go swimming with my black girlfriends. They always say, "Let's go," when it cools off. "I'm black enough," or, "I don't want my kids getting too black out there." Everyone's seems to have this "I'm black enough; don't need to be any darker" attitude. Clearly we don't need to lie out in the sun to tan. I just feel black people put too much emphasis on not wanting to be any darker.

Black women, just know that you are beautiful. We don't have to fit into anyone's image of what someone else thinks is pretty. Let's just be happy with ourselves. Sisters, don't talk about your fellow sister. We get talked about enough, and if you're one of those sisters doing the talking, because you feel you're better because you have lighter skin, then step outside yourself and really think about what you're doing. It's cruel. I believe that when you talk about someone else, it's to make yourself feel better. There must be some sort of insecurity within yourself.

There are some light skinned women out there who own their blackness, even when other people tell them they are not black enough. I mentioned this in a prior chapter. It's as if we break down our levels of blackness to fractions of a hue. Someone not being black enough versus the typical or standard looking black women. Take Mariah Carey for instance. She does not reflect a black women to me; nevertheless, she is half black, and is proud of it, which she should be. Now, let's look at someone like Halle Berry. She too is half black, however, her looks reflect more of a black women than Mariah Carey does. Halle Berry once said. "Blackness is a state of mind and I identify with the black community. Mainly because I realized early on when I walk into a room, people see a black woman; they don't see a white woman. So out of that reason alone, I identify more with the black community." When I read this, I realized that it was not easy for her in the movie industry to get roles, as opposed to someone with the white woman looks of Mariah Carey. On the other hand, it was more acceptable for her to get those roles as opposed to someone like Lauryn Hill, who is a pretty black woman with a chocolate complexion who wears natural hair. I am not putting Lauryn Hill in the same category has Halle Berry it terms of talent; I am comparing them solely on their physical characteristics. So, the more color you have, the more you are identified with black. In most cases, darker skin is not well perceived, as is reflected by Hollywood.

So when someone says you're not black enough, they're just saying you have no idea what their trials are in terms of having darker skin.

I was so astonished to find out that so many African-American women were upset by a statement made by Michelle Obama. I find her statement to be truthful and not negative. Mrs. Obama did not say she experienced racism; she said she was in another culture, a culture that was not created by her kind or mine. This is what she said. "My experiences at Princeton have made me far more aware of my blackness than ever before. I have found that at Princeton, no matter how liberal and open-minded some of my white professors and classmates try to be towards me, I sometimes feel like a visitor on a campus; as if I really don't belong, regardless of the circumstances under which I interact with whites at Princeton. It's often seems as if, to them, I will always be black and a student second."

People made comments, saying that she should be blessed that she went to Princeton and was able to get a good education. Again, that's what I call the acceptance of being accepted. To me, that is saying, "Just ignore or neglect your feelings as a human being". Did she say she wasn't blessed? There were comments made that she was admitting to inferiority and pleading for a handout; other people said she was whining about how tough the world is. White people feel as if she is delusional for feeling that way. Michelle is not the typical light-skinned African-American women that the media ponders over. She is a beautiful black woman of color who shows the world how diverse we are. My point is that Michelle is a very educated, compassionate, black woman. She is now our First Lady of the United States of America and she can admit to feeling separated in the world and should not be ashamed of admitting that it's just the way it is. Behind every good man is a good woman and we now have an African-American First Lady of the United States of America I am proud of us black women. We all need to pray for her and her husband, to guide them and give them wisdom to be great leaders of our nation. Black women, we have to love and support one another. We have a lot to be proud of.

There have been many influential black women, throughout our history, who have knocked down doors of steel when poverty, racism, sexism, and, for some of these women, mental abuse, physical abuse, and sexual abuse, stared them right in the face, telling them they can't be anything because they're poor, black, ugly, and bound by generational curses. Guess what! they believed in themselves; they believe in new song. Something all of these women have in common is that they help others through their gifts. These women include Maya Angelou, Shirley Chisholm, Harriet Tubman, Mary McLeod Bethune, Oprah Winfrey, and the list could go on. Talking about a woman who has beat all the odds, Oprah is the richest African American women of the twentieth century, and is said to be the most philanthropic African Americans of all time. She has made some enormous milestones in her life and she continues to reach even more phenomenal achievements. Be proud of who we are and what we are becoming. Thinking back on the movie. "The Color Purple", which I absolutely love – although I was all of five years old when that movie was produced, it is one of my all time favorite movies – Oprah gave a remarkable performance in that movie. Although she was nominated for an Academy Award for Best Supporting Actress she did not win, GO FIGURE. Her efforts were not in vain; she has had many more endeavors that the world was going to see. So, black women, take pride in yourselves, and be proud of where we come from and where we are going; we are headed for new dimensions. We have to renew the way we respect each other, in order for others to change the way we want them to respect us. If they shall never change, don't worry. Concentrate on you and be pleased that at least you have done your part.

Chapter Five

Our children

"The future belongs to those who give the next generation reason for hope."

Pierre Teilhard De Chardin

Our children are our future, and that is the truth. That phrase couldn't have been said any better than that. I love children; I love the purity in a child, their hilarious questions and their unconditional love, their positive energy, their will to want to learn. Children are like little sponges. They absorb whatever they hear and are not afraid to be squeezed out. We as adults, parents, and mentors have to teach and instill the very best in our children. Children need to be encouraged, loved, and supported, and it's important that they be taught to love themselves. This can have a huge impact early on in a child's life. Adults who struggle with self-esteem issues today show the adverse effects of not being taught to love themselves as children. We all know how cruel kids can be to anyone they think is different; whether you have glasses or you're overweight or if you're too light or too dark, wear no name brand shoes, etc. Kids find all kind of reasons to tease another person. It's all a part of growing up. It's what most of us call bullies; bullies have existed in schools as long as kids have been wearing backpacks. I think bullies get gratification when they see someone hurt or bothered by their actions, and when we show them that we are not affected by the taunting, they will eventually stop.

The thing that hurts me is when children are affected, and do not seem happy to be themselves, but want to be different or someone else because they think they're inadequate.

My inspiration behind this chapter comes from my very own children. I have four children, including my two stepdaughters, and I notice just how much they always talk about everyone's skin color and hair. Now I remember, as a little girl, my sister and I would wear towels on our head and pretend that it was our hair. I think every little black girl went through that phase at some point. My concern is with how much this topic was part of their day-to-day conversation. Whenever they saw a girl on television with light skin and long hair they would say, "I want to be her. She's pretty." I also noticed that they would make comments on my younger daughter's skin complexion and my husband's. They would say, "Man, Daddy, you and Sienna are dark." So my husband and I decided to have a talk with them and see where all this was coming from. The girls told us that, at their school, there were a lot of white people and most of the girls had long hair and they always asked them why they didn't wear their hair down, and they thought it was better to have light skin than dark skin. Therefore they wished they were white so people would leave them alone.

So!! as loving parents, we had to let them know that there is nothing wrong with having some color and that everyone is different. That does not mean that they are not as pretty as someone else. We let them know that they are beautiful and that God created each one of us the way he wanted us to look, and that he loves us and we should love ourselves. It's not an easy thing to always accept when the world is so critical of self-image. My sister is lighter than I am, and I used to always think she was fortunate to be light skinned. I just thought somehow that it was better, so I understand firsthand how they feel, and I know how important it is that this subject is talked about with our young ones.

Last year, my family and I lived in Jerusalem, and my son attended an international school where he was the only African American boy in the whole school. In February, his class studied black history and slavery, and being the only black child in his class, he was bombarded with questions that he did not know how to answer. So when he came home he said, "Mom, white people didn't use to like black people and they used to treat us bad." He would also say things like, "Mom, there are more white people in the world than blacks." The following year we were in Italy and people had a tendency to always stare at us because, well, there weren't many of us there. My son would get upset and say, "Man, they act like they never seen a black person before." We have now had a talk with him, because we noticed that he is always worried about race. We have to teach him to be more resilient to things people may say or do. I don't want him worrying about his color. I just want my children to be happy in their own skin. We have to pay close attention to our children's actions and words because something that we may not think is detrimental now could be later on in life. We shall bring our children up with love and wisdom and help them love and be proud of themselves, for they are our future.

As I was in the process of writing this book I decided to put a video on YouTube regarding the subject at hand. I was stunned at the response that I received; within the first month, I had over fifteen thousand viewers and an abundant number of e-mails. I was appalled?? by the number of young African American girls' responses to my video. There were also girls of other ethnicities, such as Puerto Rican and Eastern descent, all of which talked about having the same issues. These issues included being made to feel negated by their peers for having darker complexions. A few of them were having problems with boys saying cruel things with regard to their complexions as well.

If you are a young woman and you are going through something similar, please keep this in mind. God has created you as special: there is only one you; no one can be just like you. Someone may look like you or even walk, talk, or dress like you, but there is only one you. God took his time with you to make you an individual, and he loves you. Even though he created us all as individuals, he created each of us the same way. Having self confidence is the key to feeling great about yourself. If you feel like you've got it going on, then believe me, you look like you've got it going on. When you feel good about yourself and LOVE yourself, it's a reflection of yourself, and others will receive that pride from you. It's not an easy thing to do, especially if you have had someone telling you for so long that you're not good enough. Just think, if someone is trying to make you feel bad about yourself, it's a problem they have with themselves, harping over them. Remember the story about my boyfriend's mom in high school? People only scrutinize others because they have nothing else to do and they are lost or lacking something in their lives. So I want you to look in that mirror and tell yourself that you are beautiful for who you are, not for what you are not. Start conditioning your mind with a new thought. The Bible says that you are to be "transformed by the renewing of your mind." (Romans 12:12) Life is not all about looks: we all have a purpose here. Not only did God create us as special, he also gave each of us a talent and a purpose. Find your purpose and cherish yourself. Here is a famous quote that I find interesting:

"Your soul recognizes at its deepest level that everyone is the same self in different disguises" Deepak Chopra

Chapter Six

A little history

> *"History, despite its wrenching pain, cannot be unlived, but if faced with courage, need not believed again."*
>
> *Maya Angelou*

I felt that it was imperative to do a brief recap on slavery, to tie everything all together. I'm sure most of are knowledgeable of your history, but it never hurts to be reminded. There is just so much to say about slavery. That's why there are so many books out there regarding this topic. I am no history teacher, nor am I trying to be one. I just find it all very interesting and feel it's important to know where you came from. I know many black men and women who refused to watch the movie *Roots*. I know it's a hard thing to accept, but I feel the movie is very powerful; it gives you a sense of pride. Yes, I understand that it can be overwhelming and upsetting, but it's the truth and it shows how strong our culture is. We should be proud of our people and the sacrifices they made. Now we have a brighter future.

In my recent studies, I have read that some people think that the Bible condones slavery. The Bible does refer to servants and only mentions the word slave a few times. It does not mention that slavery was based on racism or a nationality and cannot be compared in any way to the history that I am about to discuss. The word of GOD would not condone such cruelties. Man always will find something to justify his wrongdoings.

Now, the first actual public or documented sale of an African slave took place, to my understanding, in Portugal, around 1444. Slave traders were sailing the west and central coast of Africa looking for what I call victims. Around the fifteenth century, the Dutch started supplying colonies in Brazil and South America. Eventually, the English got their hands dirty as well. In 1562, what has been said to be the first Englishman to take slaves from Africa was a man by the name of John Hawkins? John was a shipbuilder born in England and was quite wealthy; he collaborated with funds for a trade enterprise. Some research says that Queen Elizabeth partly helped with funds and a ship, while others say that she was not pleased by his doings. Some slave owners believed that they were doing Africans some good by introducing them to Christianity and civilization. Who says that they weren't civilized???

Slaves were then introduced to the English American colonies by a Dutch trader in 1619. They sold slaves to the settlers at Jamestown, Virginia. After that, trade between North America and Africa became an enormous enterprise, with an overall estimate of twelve million Africans shipped to the Americas between the sixteenth to the nineteenth centuries. Of these, an estimated 645,000 were brought to what is now called the United States of America. The larger numbers were shipped to Brazil or the Spanish colonies in

Central and South America. Only 6 percent were traded to British North America.

Earlier in the book, I had mentioned that most Spanish people (referring to South America) and African Americans came from one race. This is clearly why I feel that Africans helped populate their countries.

Slavery was an awful period of time; it was something that was going on all over the world. We have come a long way, not withstanding all the detestation our culture has persevered— the pain, torture, suffering, hatred, self-hatred—but we are emerging. However, we still use slave-minded mentalities against one another. These actions also can be traced back almost three hundred years ago, with something called Willie Lynch syndrome. Willie Lynch was a slave owner in the West Indies who was invited to Virginia to teach slave owners his methods. Willie Lynch devised a plan that would keep black people divided. He believed that the hangings of Negro slaves were a waste, because they were losing valuable crops and many slaves were running away. Since their crops were being left in the field too long to maximize profit, he wanted to gain mental control over his slaves. His plan was simple: he said he would use FEAR, DISTRUST, and ENVY for control purposes. One of his main focuses was to cause dissention by pitching the old black slaves against the young black males. He also incited factions between the young and the old, the dark skinned slaves and the light skinned slaves, and the males and the females. What I find most thought-provoking is that he said, "I guarantee everyone of you that, if instilled correctly, it will control all slaves for at least three hundred years, maybe thousands." Sorrowfully, we see that some of us are still controlled by this awful conditioned mindset right now today, two hundred and ninety seven years later. Ironically, there has been some speculation on the authenticity of the Willie Lynch letter, which is said to be a verbatim copy of a speech he gave. This speech appeared on the internet as early as 1993. In our culture today, the Willie Lynch syndrome is taught by some college professors and it continues to appear in books, songs, and even movies. In the movie the Great Debaters with Denzel Washington, his character refers to the Willie Lynch speech as being the definition of the black slave. In my opinion, whether or not this document is authentic, whether or not Willie Lynch said it or another slave owner thought it, this deception, manipulation and torment was done to us. As a result, our culture is still divided by these true or false theories. We cannot blame all of our problems on one white man's theory. On the contrary, black slavery was atrocious, and in my opinion, years of oppression will take years to undo.

So, my people, let's get busy because we still have work to do and battles to win. We have made great strides but it is not all said and done. We have to work on ourselves before we can change the mindsets of others. That's my goal: to change mindsets one book at a time. I hope this information has enlightened those of you who were left in the dark about this subject. We need to look at our struggles and make some positive changes for our culture.

I think of how proud the great Martin Luther King would be right now, to see that we are free and so much more. In the words of Dr. Martin Luther King's "I have a dream" speech:

> "I have a dream that one day this nation will rise up and live out the meaning of its creed: 'We will hold these truths to be self-evident that all men are created equal.'"

We can proudly say that, in 2009, we have witnessed an historical moment in history, something that many of us, young and old, thought we would never see. Some people tried very hard to prevent him from being the President; they made his words sound negative even when he was clearly positive. Lower-class Caucasians said they'd rather be poor than support a nigger. It was said that it would not be possible for a black man to be President. Contrary to the fact that our newly elected President is African American, the fact remains that racism is still amongst us. I'm not saying everyone is a racist, but merely recognizing that it still exists.

America has an unsettling track record of moral failures by some of our nation's influential leaders, Presidents, and most Americans. America is Notorious for its diversity. No matter how we look at it, we all emerged here either voluntarily or involuntarily, and are all considered as American. Nonetheless, this is where it gets complicated; we are all characterized by our ethnic origins and placed in categories. There are so many different bubbles to fill in when applying for a job. African American, Native American, Mexican American, white, Asian, and et cetera. We all originated from our homelands, obviously. However, most African Americans were born in America and most have never been to Africa; most have no desire to go to Africa. So we don't understand how our culture operates. The majority of young people today could not care less about embracing their culture. I find that other nationalities are more in synch with their culture for one reason; most of them travel back to their homelands and have a profound comprehension of what their culture is about. Some are just immigrating to the United States and they come with their cultural beliefs and values. Culture encompasses the broad spectrum of ways in which we define ourselves, such as values, traditions, shared beliefs, and customs.

I feel that every race has prejudice and even develops subordinate behaviors amongst themselves. I am not trying to single out one nationality over another; I am just trying to make a valid point. I use situations and conversations with others to make my analogies. Now take Ethiopians, for an example. I had a friend whose father despised African Americans; he felt we were unintelligent, irrational, and immoral. He looked down on us, as if it was our fault that we were stripped from our culture and had to adapt to the white man's culture. Ethiopians have strong family values and beliefs and that is a magnificent thing. Regardless of how you view yourself, you shouldn't look down on others for not having the morals and values you possess. This goes for African Americans in the United States who live better than those in the projects. You look down on them because they're not as privileged as you are; they're called ghetto, or ignorant. This also holds for Caucasians; you have subordinates as well – you call yours white trash. Hispanics in the United States that are doing well call their own wetbacks, and the list goes on. You see, we all have some prejudice in each of our cultures. So before we dismiss each other, let's recollect the thought that we are all products of our environment. We will imitate whatever culture we are raised around. So unless we are going to educate ourselves on another's culture, we shouldn't pass judgments or think of ourselves as the superior race. That's how racism began: the Europeans were in a race to be superior and found it expedient to make white the subject of grandness and they were able to persuade man to think that they were better than the blacks.

Even with such imperfections, I never hated my country. Given our newly elected President, I am proud to see change in our country, and I am proud to be an American. I do not just like Barack because he is black; I feel like he will be stupendous leader. I am proud that he is black. I think it's quite a courageous aspiration to want to be the President of the United States; for any man, woman, or child to have that dream is bewildering.

President Barak Obama has received many death threats throughout his campaign. I'm sure that there have been situations where the President may have felt petrified. I feel that he has an enormous amount of pressure on him, more than any other President of our time. Not only is he the fifth youngest President, as if that isn't enough pressure, you also have to factor in his skin color. People are going to be watching him as if under a microscope and scrutinizing his every action and word. The impression I get of Obama is of someone who is not only highly intelligent but street smart, for lack of a better word. He is someone who understands, and is not oblivious to the fact of how some people perceive him. He realizes he is only human and is not perfect. He has openly talked about real life situations in the past that have proven him not to be perfect. Previous Presidents have tried to hide their imperfections, as if this isn't life and you aren't faced with trials and temptations. This standpoint alone exhilarates me to respect him even more. So, with a person like this, he is expecting the unexpected and I believe he will triumph through the obstacles to fight for what he believes in. Some people are always afraid of change. Literally!

As I have mentioned a couple of times before, I travel to and from Europe frequently. Earlier this year, December to be exact, I flew to Germany on my way back home to the United States. I was a flustered mess, my incoming flight into Germany arrived late, leaving me with fifteen minutes to board my International connecting flight. That is not even enough time to board a domestic flight, and all that I could think of at this point was how devastated I would be if I missed the flight. As I was running through the crowed airport that reeked of cigarette smoke, weaving around people while I was pushing a stroller, holding onto my carry-on luggage and trying to managing my eight year old son, I finally made it to passport control with three minutes before the plane would board. I was tired and out of breath, my heart was beating immensely because of the anxiety of the thought that I was going to stuck in Germany for ten hours. There were about ten or more people in front of me. I hesitated to ask if I could go ahead of them, if their plane was not yet leaving, because of the fact that I could not tell if they spoke English or not. When I realized that this should not be a thought and how desperate I was to board this flight, I immediately started asking people in the back of the line if I could go ahead, because my flight was leaving in a couple of minutes. People were very friendly and allowed my children and me to pass. There was a nice looking Caucasian family of four in front of me; before I could even ask, the man said "Are you trying to board the flight to Chicago?" I said "No, I'm going to Los Angeles." He replied "Well, you need to wait like everyone else. I don't know what wrong with you people, ain't nothing changed." I won't even write the thoughts that were running through my head. However, I said, "What the…I can't believe you just said that. Wow. I knew there were still people like you out there."

I can't tell you why things of this magnitude ALWAYS happen to me. I have experienced racism and been in prejudiced situations ever since I can remember. Usually individuals with these stories have lived a lot longer than I have. I've asked my husband if he has ever experienced any type of racial experiences and he has said no, not that he can remember. All

I can say is that God must be doing something in me, because I have really learned how to shrug people off in most situations. That's why I can write this book, in truth, because I have experienced my share of things. I am a very analytical person; when people think I'm not paying any attention to them, I usually am. So despite the fact that there are a tremendous number of good people out there, willing and ready to make some changes, there are also many who won't accept it. So, in the words of President Obama......

> "Change will not come if we wait for some other person or some other time. We are the ones we've been waiting for. We are the change that we seek."

God makes all things possible to those who believe, and Mr. Barack Obama is inspiration to many.

Chapter Seven

In Summation

All that you have read are worldly issues that we face because we allow the thoughts of others to affect our lives. We allow our past to define us and we allow our superficial ways to determine who we are. We need to become a prodigy of God and thrive off of love and the willingness to love and be kind and understanding. Here are some key points that have been talked about in this book:

1. Love yourself for who you are, not for what you're not.

If you could afford a skin transplant, if there were such thing, to change your color or perhaps if you could change the appearance of your features, would you be happier? I don't think so, because your soul is still the same. You should learn to love yourself from within. Life is too short to be focused on appearance. Inner beauty will take you much farther than outward beauty; your outer beauty can be hindered by numerous reasons. So shine from within. Besides, you're beautiful.

2. Don't accept the acceptance of being accepted.

Please don't let anyone make you feel like you're better than someone else, because they perceive you as being lucky. Lucky for not looking like the people, who they find to be less unfortunate. You give them reason to believe their prejudice, thinking it justifiable.

3. Be a good role model.

Don't forget about those young ones who are watching our actions; the way we think of ourselves and the way we treat and perceive others. They're soaking it all in and that will shape the outcome of the way they see themselves.

This can be something as small as looking in the mirror and saying "I'm fat" or "I'm too dark I wish I was lighter". This can be said unintentionally, because you're accustomed to thinking this way, and your thoughts have now become words. You need to realize that there is someone around whose mind is so innocent that you can start shaping their thoughts into believing they should not be a certain image.

4. Start changing your mindset.

Start renewing your mind today! This goes for all people, whatever the issue. If you're the girl with the low self esteem, because the world has been so critical of you, today you start thinking, walking, and talking differently. You are only what you think you are; change begins with you. You are beautiful.

If you're the one that's been judging, STOP! You're not God and you will be judged soon. Stop being so superficial, and get over yourself, please!!! No one is perfect and no race is better than the next. We are all God's people. And we are all a product of our environment. We can't help the way we were raised, but we can learn from the negative circumstances we have faced; we can take the negative energy and simply divert it into something positive start helping and stop hating.

What you are about to read are real letters from individuals who are struggling with some of these same issues. I received these e-mails after I posted my video blog on YouTube. I wanted to see the response that I would get from this topic, and I am pleased with the outcome and the people that it has touched. Some of these individuals wanted to remain anonymous. I think it was very courageous for these individuals to speak openly and honestly; saying things that some of you think; but will never admit. These letters were very inspirational to me, as my video was to them. I always felt that there was a need to discuss this issue and I am overwhelmed by the number of people from every nationality that responded. So I want to thank each of you for allowing me to read your stories and allowing me to share with others too, showing them that they are not alone.

Acurrylady,

My name is annyonmous and I'm seventeen years old. All my life, I've had male friends tell me, "I like Asian girls only." Or I've heard some of my girl friends who are not black say," Black girls don't have nice hair because it's thin; some don't have much hair at all." Sadly, some guys won't even look in my direction because of one thing....my brown skin. I mainly live in a Caucasian and Asian predominant area. Even the few blacks we have here won't give me the time of day. Guys will look at my friends but I feel invisible to them. The fact that you are writing a book makes me look up to you, and opens my mind to the fact that, it's not me with the problem. It has been the people around me with the problem. I've been told "You're pretty for a black girl" or "You're pretty for a ebony girl" I once responded "there are many beautiful black women in this world, as much as a lot of other beautiful women in other races." I don't understand how people can limit their minds so much to believing a certain race is ugly? Your video has made me feel happy and beautiful. I will read your book when I feel down about myself to be reminded that I am not alone. Thank you.

Aisha,

I have just watched both of your videos and BRAVO to you for your brave effort. I look forward to your book when it comes out. I have never had the pleasure of hearing the words "You're pretty for a black girl" So; I guess that means I must be pretty ugly. I know that personally I think I am, but I was born that way and I can't really change it and I don't have the money to get the plastic surgeries I would like to get (primarily getting my nose narrowed.)

I have always hated my color. At 43years, I still have moments when I wish I was born white, so I could be seen as beautiful and desirable. I grew up never wanting to marry anyone black because I wanted my kids to be light skin and have "good" hair. So, guess what, I am still single. Young black females today have it a little better than I did growing up. At least you have some black images to look up to, such as actresses, ad models, and others like Oprah Winfrey. Growing up in early 70's, I didn't have that. I didn't grow up in a home where you heard that "black was beautiful" either. The only person I ever heard anyone called beautiful in my family was my cousin and she was so fair she could pass for white; everyone loved her.

The only thing about myself I have learned to love is my hair. I went natural 15yrs ago and I love it. Now my hair is strong and grows like I wished it would have grown when I was a child. I recently decided to lock it just for something different. As far as attractive or pretty, I have accepted that I am not and never will be. Especially in a world where the only beauty that is valued is that of a white women. Accepting this helps me to stop stressing about it and just live my life. I just felt the need to share my feelings.   Kiki S.

Hi Aisha,

I really liked both of your vids coz I thought they were so true. I felt like I could relate in a lot of ways. I'm actually of East Indian descent, but born and raised in America. I wasn't raised with any of that Indian culture and when I grew up and tried to be friends with Indian people, they shunned me because I am, for their standards, dark and have thick, coarse curly hair, big lips and a big nose, all of which Indian people consider very ugly. To them, I look like a "low caste girl" and my father is from the lower caste, but I don't have anything to do with him or his family and I really don't care what the Indian people think of me anymore. I don't associate with them. Most people consider me; by the way I dress, to be gothic. I don't like labels, but you get the idea. I don't really date white guys, though, because most white Goth guys only like the very pale, vampire looking girls. Plus, I've always been attracted to black guys since I was 9 so I've mostly only been with black guys and Latinos. And let me tell you, it disgusts me when some have told me that they prefer white women to black women, because I consider myself more or less part of a black race and I'm like, "Hey dude are you trying to tell me something about myself?" I've then asked them why that is and a few said something about straight hair, but interestingly most of them said it's because of attitude. These guys have always been the ones who grew up around mostly white people and only saw a few black women who fit the "hood rat" stereotype. Perhaps they weren't telling me the whole truth, but they seem to have stereotyped black women just as badly as white people have. BTW, I graduated from an HBCU and had lots of friends who were super-classy, intelligent, beautiful black women, so I know this isn't true. As for me, I definitely don't think I'm better than black women. In fact, if I had a choice, I'd rather be black than Indian. At one time, I wore my hair in long cornrows, dressed in hip hop name brands, and told people I was black. I definitely got more guys when I was "black" than I ever did being Indian. In fact, there were a few black guys who I lied about my race to and when they found out what I really was, they didn't wanna speak to me anymore. Well, keep it real girl. Sorry this is so long, lol. But that's my input. Hope it was helpful in some way.

- Anyonoumos

Hi Aisha,

I just wanted to take the time to write a quick note in response to your video posts. As a white man who just happens to have and will continue to date outside my race, I have some experience in ignorance from all races. The statement made to you in the convenience store was unfortunately obliviously racist. What I mean is, if you ask those people, in their heart they probably don't believe that are bigots. They are. Anytime you lump any group of people together or paint them with one broad stroke, you just happen to be closed minded and usually an elitist. Being in interracial relationships, especially here in the south, puts you and your loved one in the direct path for anyone who happens to be closed off from the rest of the world or to their immediate surroundings. I'll tell ya though, from my own experience, I take away the open minded non racist looks and actions more than I ever will the contentment or venom thrown.

-Rob-